How to Draw
Scary
Monsters
and Other Mythical Creatures

sourcebooks
wonderland

Created and produced by Green Android Ltd

Illustrated by Fiona Gowen

First edition for The United States and Canada
published in 2017 by
Barron's Educational Series, Inc.

This edition for The United States and Canada
published in 2023 by Sourcebooks Wonderland,
an imprint of Sourcebooks Kids
P.O. Box 4410, Naperville, Illinois 60567-4410
(630) 961-3900
sourcebookskids.com

Copyright © Green Android Ltd 2017
Green Android Ltd
49 Beaumont Court
Upper Clapton Road
London E5 8BG
United Kingdom
www.greenandroid.co.uk

ISBN 978-1-4380-1055-7

Source of Production:
Toppan Leefung Printing Co., Ltd.,
Shenzhen, China
Date of Production: April 2023
Run Number: 5030576

Printed and bound in China.
GA 10 9 8 7 6 5 4 3 2

Contents

Page 32 has an index of everything to draw in this book.

How to Draw

Wicked Vampire

Folklore says that vampires live forever by feeding on human blood. Garlic and holy water can ward them off, and they can be destroyed by a stake through the heart.

1 Sketch the vampire's head and the outline of his cape.

2 Draw the front of the cape and the vampire's pant legs.

3 Add a vest with small circles for the buttons. Draw shoes and a tall collar on the cape.

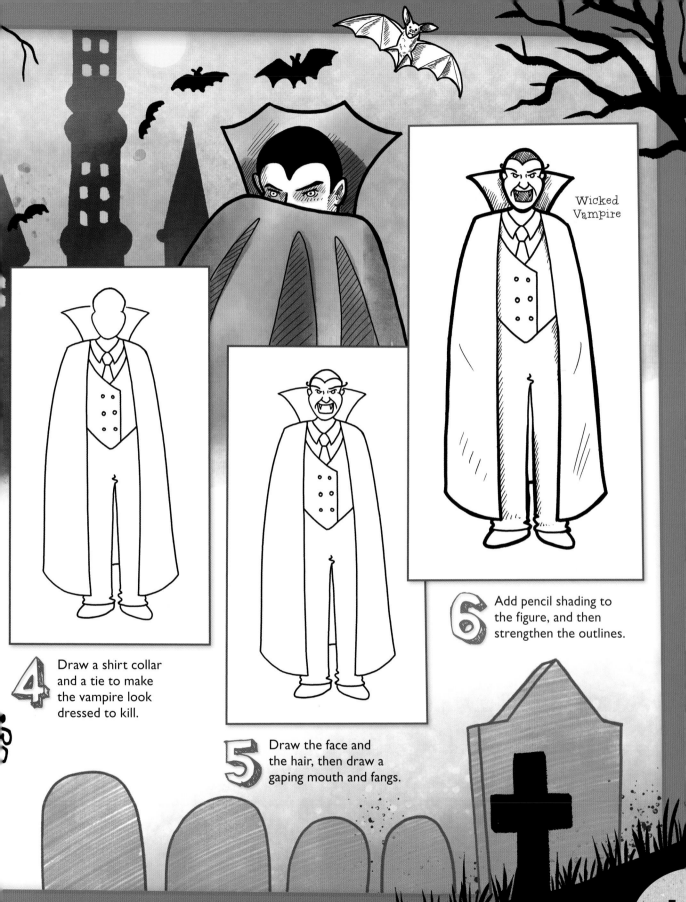

Wicked Vampire

4 Draw a shirt collar and a tie to make the vampire look dressed to kill.

5 Draw the face and the hair, then draw a gaping mouth and fangs.

6 Add pencil shading to the figure, and then strengthen the outlines.

How to Draw

Bull-headed Minotaur

The Minotaur of Greek mythology was a creature with the head of a bull and the body of a man. He lived in the center of a labyrinth and liked to eat humans.

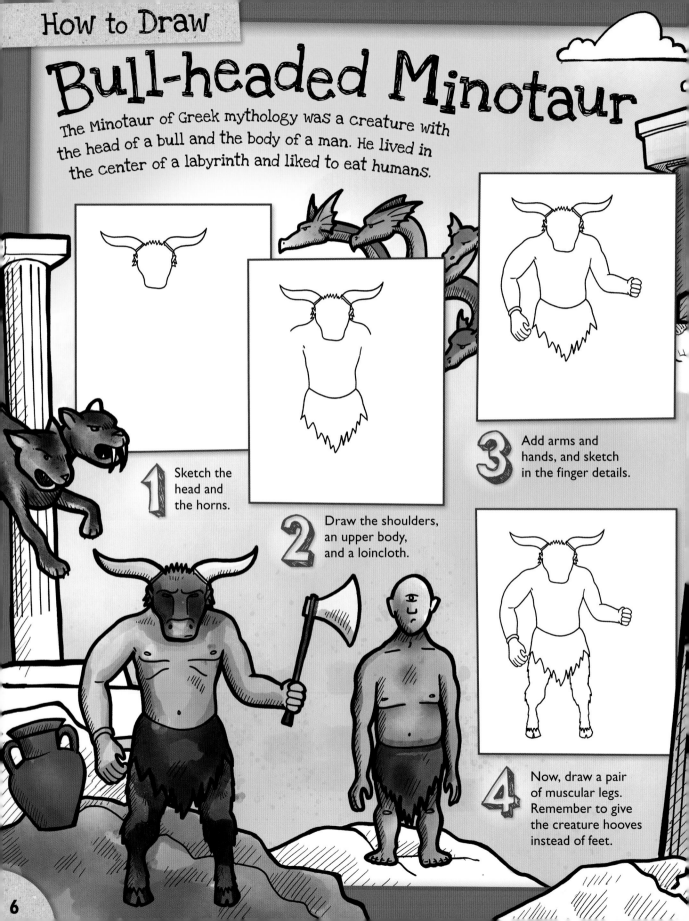

1 Sketch the head and the horns.

2 Draw the shoulders, an upper body, and a loincloth.

3 Add arms and hands, and sketch in the finger details.

4 Now, draw a pair of muscular legs. Remember to give the creature hooves instead of feet.

Ichthyocentaur

Centaur

Orthrus

Chimera

5 Add detail to the face and the body. Then, draw an axe.

Cyclops

Hydra

Bull-headed Minotaur

Ophiotaurus

6 Add shading, and then strengthen the outlines.

Satyr

How to Draw

Cave Troll

Large, awkward, and unintelligent cave trolls appear in Norse mythology. Folklore claims that they are frightened of lightning and church bells!

1 Draw the head, spiky hair, long beard, and shoulders.

2 Pencil two vertical lines for the trunk, and draw a loincloth.

3 Add two strong arms with hands and fingers.

4 Draw short, muscular legs and large, broad feet.

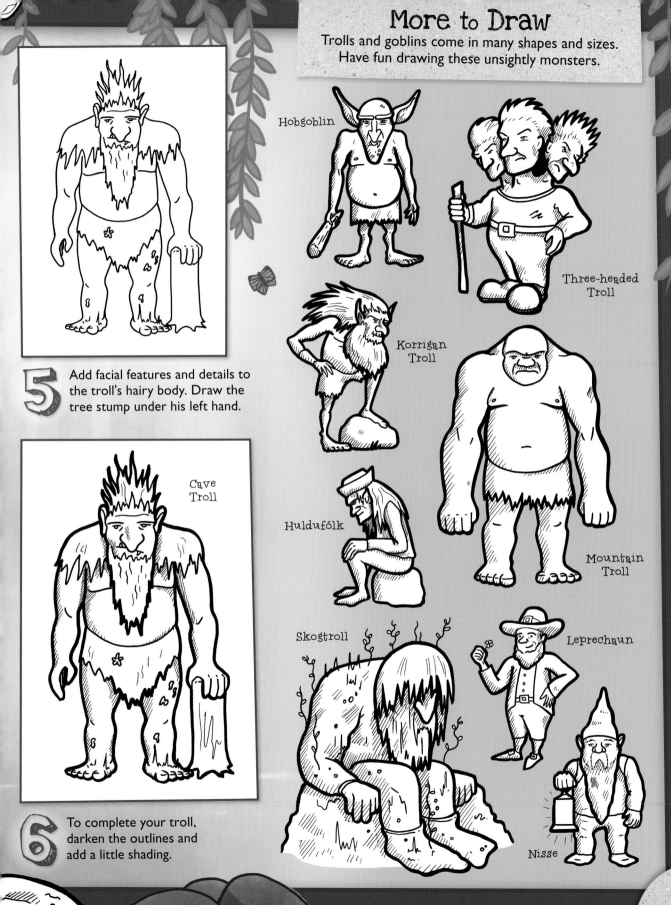

More to Draw

Trolls and goblins come in many shapes and sizes. Have fun drawing these unsightly monsters.

5 Add facial features and details to the troll's hairy body. Draw the tree stump under his left hand.

6 To complete your troll, darken the outlines and add a little shading.

Cave Troll

Hobgoblin

Three-headed Troll

Korrigan Troll

Huldufólk

Mountain Troll

Skogtroll

Leprechaun

Nisse

How to Draw
Fearsome Dragon

This legendary creature can breathe fire. It has scales like a reptile, moves like a snake, and flies like a bird. In stories, only the bravest of knights can face a dragon.

1 Draw the head, pointed ear, horn, and teeth. Then, draw the neck, chest, belly, and one wing.

2 Sketch in detail to the fanlike wing. Draw the spiralling tail with its arrowhead tip.

3 Add the pointed tongue, and then draw the hind legs, feet, and taloned claws.

4 Draw the front legs complete with claws, and add in the second wing and the ear.

More to Draw

Wawel Dragon

Fafnir Dragon

Zmaj Dragon

Apalala Dragon

5 Pencil the spiny ridge on the dragon's neck, and add details and markings to the body and the tail.

Zilant Dragon

Nâga Dragon

Fearsome Dragon

Yellow Dragon

Piasa Bird

6 Use shading and darker lines to complete the picture and to make your dragon unique.

11

How to Draw

Loch Ness Monster

Some people believe that a sea monster lurks in the depths of Loch Ness, a lake in Scotland. Many have spent years trying to spot the monster they call "Nessie."

1 Draw the head, face, and slightly curved neck.

2 Add the chest, belly, and looped tail. Leave gaps for the flippers.

3 Pencil in the front flippers.

4 Add the downward pointing hind flippers.

More to Draw

Sea monster legends span from the freezing Arctic ocean to the warm Mediterranean Sea.

Scylla

Afanc

5 Draw some markings on the body, and add a ridge to its back.

Loch Ness Monster

Morgawr

Qalupalik

Makara

Selkie

6 Complete your picture with shading, and strengthen the outlines.

Tlanchi

How to Draw

Abominable Snowman

In Nepalese folklore, this creature, also known as a yeti, is apelike and tall. Some people claim to have seen a yeti or spotted its tracks in the snow.

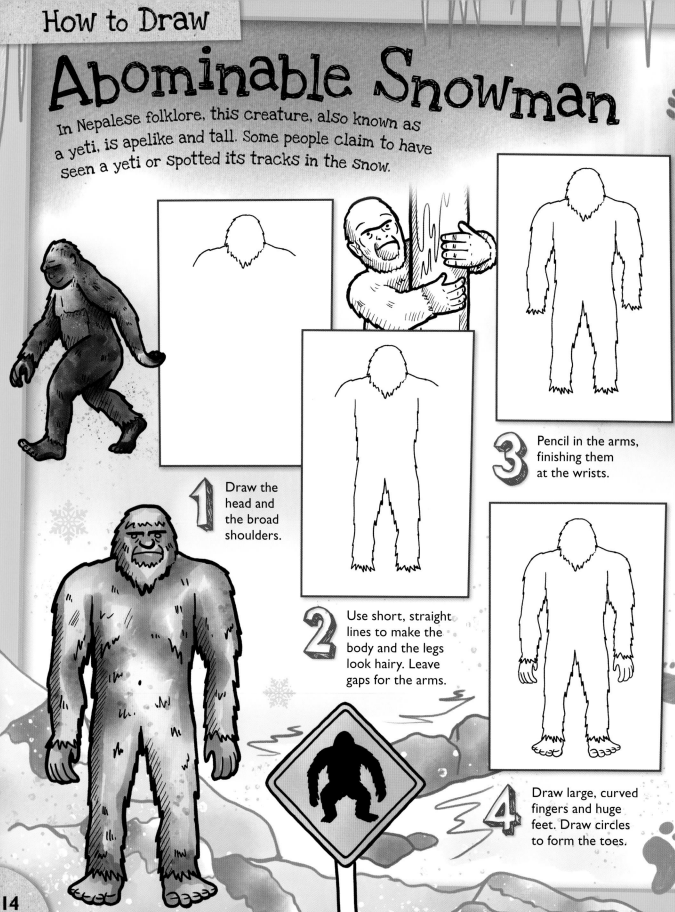

1 Draw the head and the broad shoulders.

2 Use short, straight lines to make the body and the legs look hairy. Leave gaps for the arms.

3 Pencil in the arms, finishing them at the wrists.

4 Draw large, curved fingers and huge feet. Draw circles to form the toes.

There are legends aplenty of upright-walking beasts that resemble humans and other primates.

Kikomba

Batutut

Hibagon

Big Gray Man

5 Use curved lines to give it a stomach. Add fur and a stern face.

Amomongo

Abominable Snowman

Bigfoot

Yowie

6 Add shading to one side of the body and to the limbs. Strengthen the outlines.

Orang Pendek

How to Draw

Sacred Phoenix

In Greek mythology, a phoenix dies in a blaze of flame and is reborn from the ashes. Some texts say that the cycle repeats every 1,400 years!

1 Draw a head, a curved chest, an eye, and a hooked beak.

2 Add a raised wing. Use lots of wavy lines to show that it is layered and feathery.

3 Draw the legs. Finish them to look like ragged pants. Add feet and claws.

4 Sketch the tail. At first it should look feathery, but then it should start to resemble flames.

More to Draw

Birds in legends can represent many things, from freedom and love to war and destruction.

5 Add the second wing and the head feathers. Draw tear shapes to create the tail feathers.

6 Finish by lightly shading the body, wings, and tail. Strengthen the outlines.

Sacred Phoenix

Griffin

Firebird

Gandaberunda

Garuda

Liver Bird

Harpy

Gamayun

Fenghuang

How to Draw
Warrior Ogre

These monsters of legend are usually seen as ugly, tall, and strong. They dislike human beings and are known to eat them. They most often appear in fairy tales.

1 Draw a circular head, a face, and round shoulders. Then, draw the upper body.

2 Sketch the chest, and add the warrior's armor.

3 Draw bent arms and clenched fists. Add wristguards and shoulder pads.

4 Draw thick legs set wide apart to form an "A" shape. Don't forget the feet.

Warrior Ogre

5 Draw the spiked club and the leather straps of his chest guard. Sketch lines to indicate the ground.

6 Give the ogre bulk by adding shading, and then strengthen the outlines.

Sea God Neptune

This Roman god of freshwater and the sea was also worshipped as a god of horses by the Roman people. The god Poseidon is his Greek counterpart.

1 Draw the head, face, and shoulders. Then add detail.

2 Use simple, light strokes to draw the upper body.

3 Draw one arm by his side and the other bent, with clenched fingers.

4 Complete the body, with flowing curves that lead to a webbed tail fin.

5 Give Neptune his trident —a three-pronged staff —and add scales to his fishlike lower body.

6 Lightly shade Neptune, and then strengthen the outlines.

Sea God
Neptune

How to Draw
Walking Zombie

Haitian folklore is rich with tales of the walking undead —reincarnated corpses—that attack the living. The corpses are made undead by voodoo sorcerers.

1 Draw the head, face, and shoulders using short, jagged lines.

2 Continue using sharp, hard lines for the torso. Add horizontal lines to give shape to the body.

3 Draw the legs with the knees and feet pointing inward.

4 Draw the arms at an awkward angle, and add hands with splayed fingers.

More to Draw

Zombies in all their various guises are not real although many believe differently.

5 Add rips, cuts, and dirt to the body and clothes.

Walking Zombie

6 Shade the inside of the gaping mouth and other areas of the body and limbs. Strengthen the outlines.

Escapee Zombie

Limbless Zombie

Shuffler Zombie

Creeper Zombie

Screamer Zombie

Spitter Zombie

Runner Zombie

Slime Zombie

Crawler Zombie

23

How to Draw
Howling Werewolf

This mythological beast is actually a human being who can turn into a wolflike creature. Some cultures believe that one sign of being a werewolf is curved fingernails.

1 Draw the head and the face. Note the gaping mouth and sharp teeth.

2 Add a jagged line above the head for shoulders, and add more for the torso.

3 Keep your lines jagged to show rough fur, and add two menacing arms and claws.

4 Use oval shapes to give the impression of bent legs. The knee of the forward leg should be level with the claws.

Howling Werewolf

6 Shade the werewolf's body and the inside of his mouth. Strengthen the outlines.

5 Sketch the feet. They are long and broad.

How to Draw
Curse of the Mummy

A mummy is a human or animal who has died and been preserved. They have been found all around the world, but it is only in stories that they can come back to life.

1 Draw a circle resting on a slightly curved line for the head and the shoulders.

2 Add two vertical lines for the torso, and mark the place where the legs will begin.

3 Draw the legs and add square shapes to form the feet.

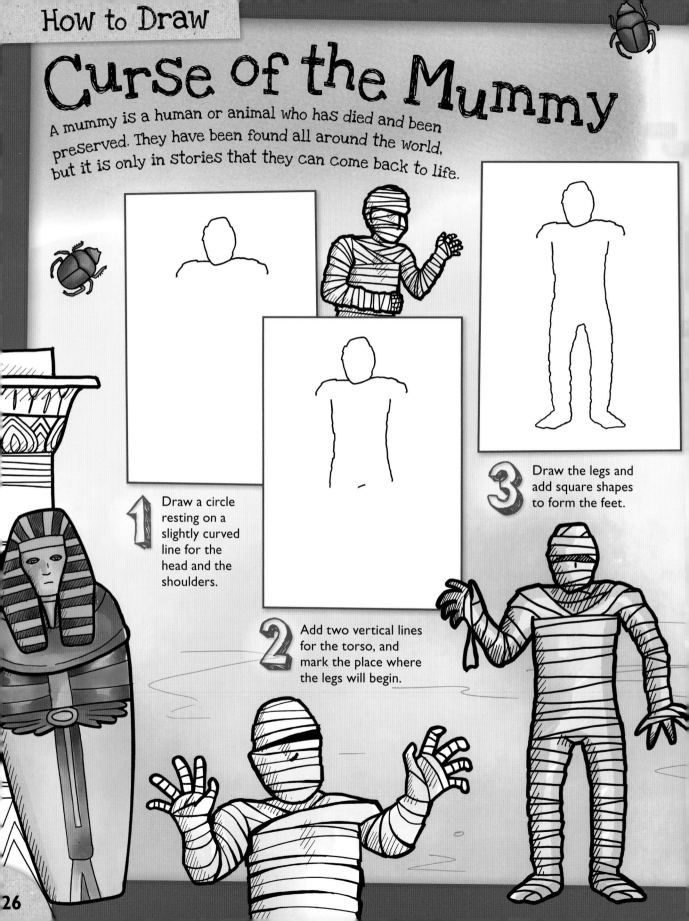

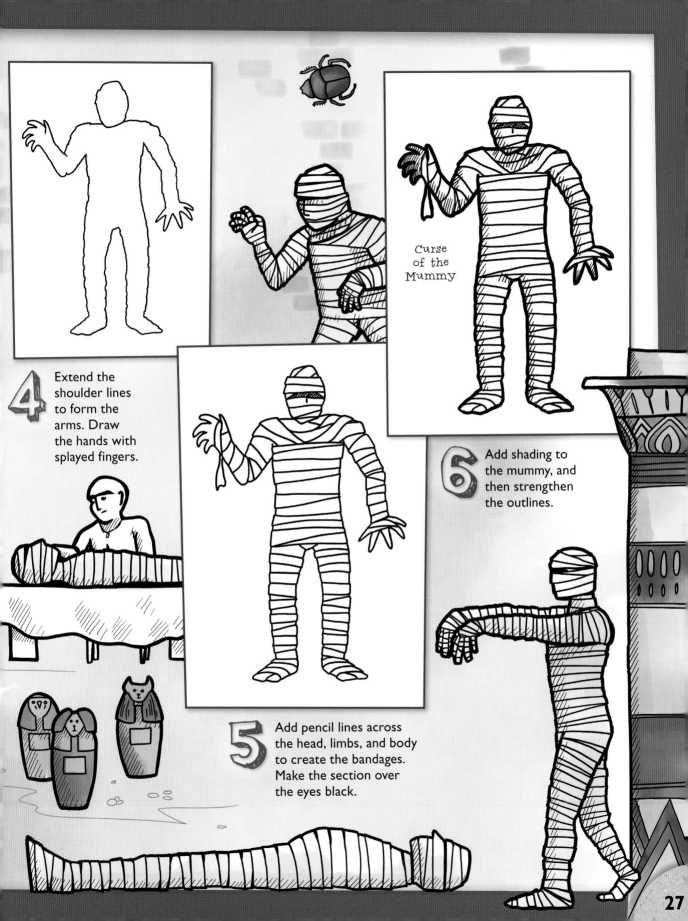

4 Extend the shoulder lines to form the arms. Draw the hands with splayed fingers.

Curse
of the
Mummy

6 Add shading to the mummy, and then strengthen the outlines.

5 Add pencil lines across the head, limbs, and body to create the bandages. Make the section over the eyes black.

Frankenstein's Monster

This fictional character was created by Mary Shelley in 1818, in her novel *Frankenstein*. He was built in a laboratory and is terrifyingly ugly but very sensitive.

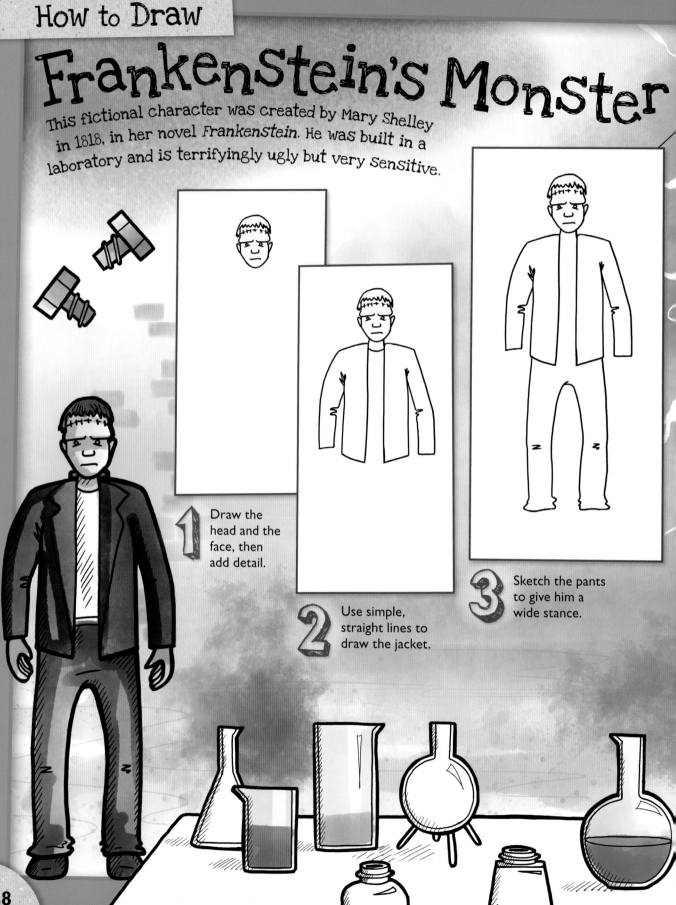

1 Draw the head and the face, then add detail.

2 Use simple, straight lines to draw the jacket.

3 Sketch the pants to give him a wide stance.

4 Draw the T-shirt neck and jacket lapels. Add short lines under the arms and at the elbows.

5 Darken the creases and add hands and feet. Now draw neck bolts.

Frankenstein's Monster

6 Shade in the body and darken the outlines of this fearsome creation.

How to Draw

Flying Pegasus

This famous winged horse exists in ancient Greek mythology. He is a horse god and even has a constellation named after him. Pegasus is a symbol of loyalty and bravery.

1 Draw the head, neck, and chest. Detail the ears and face.

2 Sketch the curly mane and a raised foreleg and hoof. Draw the belly.

3 Draw the back end, and add a hind leg and a hoof. Note the angles that make up the leg.

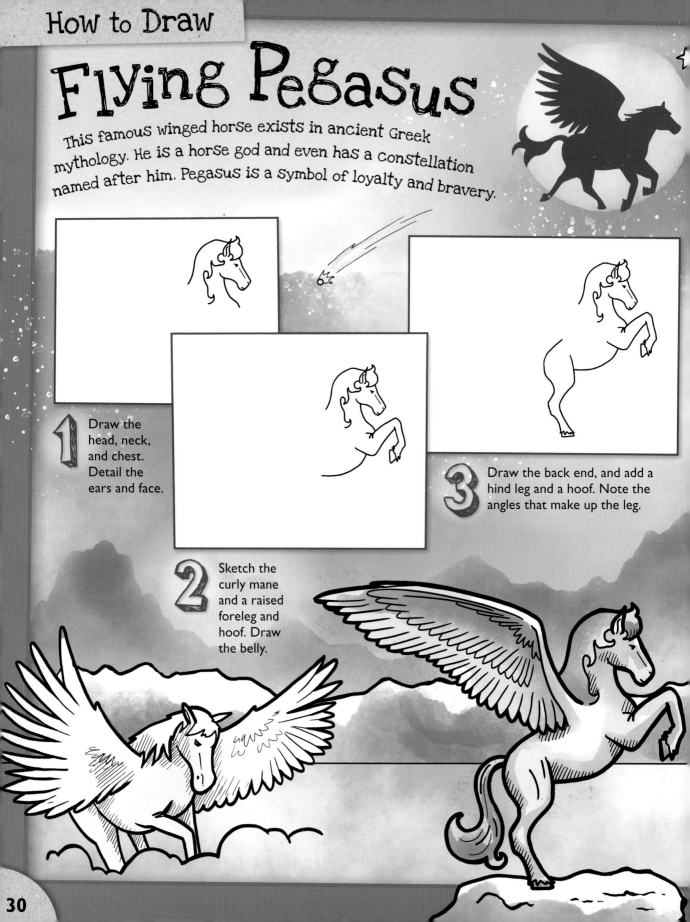

4 Sketch the outline shape of a wing, and then fill in with rows of feathers.

5 Give Pegasus a thick, flowing tail with curls that match his mane.

Flying Pegasus

6 Finish by shading the body, limbs, and wing, and then strengthen the outlines.

Index

This index is in alphabetical order, and it lists all the mythological beasts that are in this book so that you can easily find your favorites.